GOOD ST. ANNE

HER POWER AND DIGNITY

Patroness of Christian Mothers

> *"Her children rose up, and called her blessed."*
> —Proverbs 31:10, 28

TAN BOOKS AND PUBLISHERS, INC.
Rockford, Illinois 61105

Nihil obstat: William J. Blacet, J.C.L.
                  Censor Librorum

Imprimatur: ✝ John P. Cody, S.T.D.
                  Bishop of Kansas City-St. Joseph
                  December 4, 1957

Originally published by the Benedictine Convent of Perpetual Adoration, Clyde, Missouri in 1958. Revised edition published in 1963. Retypeset and re-published by TAN Books and Publishers, Inc. in 1998. Updates and additions made to information on shrines by the Publisher, 1998.

Library of Congress Catalog Card No.: 98-61404

ISBN 0-89555-641-3

Printed and bound in the United States of America.

TAN BOOKS AND PUBLISHERS, INC.
P.O. Box 424
Rockford, Illinois 61105
1998

GOOD
ST. ANNE

"And may you see your children, and your children's children, unto the third and fourth generation: and may your seed be blessed by the God of Israel, who reigneth for ever and ever. . . . Amen."
—Tobias 9:11-12

THE EDUCATION OF THE VIRGIN

On the scroll is the famous prophecy of *Isaias* 11:1:
"*Et ingredietur virga de radice Iesse . . .*"—"And there shall
come forth a rod out of the root of Jesse . . ."

"To St. Anne, God has given the power to aid in every necessity, because Jesus, her Divine Grandchild according to the flesh, will refuse her no petition, and Mary, her glorious daughter, supports her every request. Those who venerate good St. Anne shall want for nothing, either in this life or the next. . . ."

—Abbot Trithemius

CONTENTS

GOOD
ST. ANNE

"We beseech Thee, O Lord our God, that through the intercession of blessed Anne, whom Thou didst choose to be the mother of her who brought forth Thy Son, we may become worthy to win eternal salvation. Through Jesus Christ Our Lord."

—From the Postcommunion
Mass for the Feast of St. Anne
July 26

Good St. Anne

DIGNITY AND SANCTITY
OF ST. ANNE

HOW holy must have been the woman in whom the great mystery of the Immaculate Conception was accomplished! How holy the womb into which the fullness of grace descended, in which the child "full of grace" was conceived and took flesh! Great was the dignity of St. Elizabeth, the mother of St. John the Baptist, who was privileged to have her son sanctified in her womb; but how much greater is the dignity of St. Anne, whose child, by a special prerogative, from the first instant of her conception was preserved from all taint of sin! Holy was the root from which sprouted the tree that bore the holiest Fruit, Jesus. St. Anne's sanctity was increased still more through this wonderful conception: and indeed, how highly must she have been sanctified who bore the Mother of God!

Is it any wonder that **St. Jerome** praises her in the words: "Anne is the glorious tree from which bloomed a twig under divine influence. She is the

1

sublime heaven from whose heights the Star of the Sea neared its rising. She is the blessed barren woman, happy mother among mothers, from whose pure womb came forth the shining temple of God, the sanctuary of the Holy Ghost, the Mother of God!"

Yes, great indeed was the privilege and dignity conferred by God on St. Anne in electing her to be the mother of the treasury of all graces! How great must have been St. Anne's joy, how blissful her delight, when, contrary to all hope, she gave birth to a child! And what a child! Never before had earth beheld a child so fair and noble as Anne's infant daughter, "conceived without stain of Original Sin." Never had there been a maternity so rich in blessings as hers—she who was privileged to call her child by the exalted title of "Mother of God."

Well indeed might **St. John Damascene**, a great Doctor of the Church, exclaim: "Blessed, thrice blessed art thou, O Saint Anne, who didst receive from God and bring forth the blessed child from whom proceeded Christ, the Flower of life! We congratulate thee, O blessed Anne, on the dignity of being the mother of Mary, for thou hast brought forth our common hope, the germ of Promise! All pious lips bless thee in thy daughter, all languages glorify thy child! Worthy art thou above all praise, worthy of the praise of all who are redeemed, for thou hast given life to her who brought forth our Saviour, Jesus Christ."

Even her name "Anne" signifies "gracious, loving" and typifies her sublime destiny. She too had been chosen by God from eternity, and to her, as to her daughter, Mary, may be applied the words: "The Lord possessed me in the beginning of His ways . . . I was set up from eternity." (*Prov.* 8:22-23). God prepared St. Anne with magnificent gifts and graces. Of her may be said what **St. Bernardine of Siena** wrote of St. Joseph: "In the kingdom of grace the universal rule is: If God elects anyone for a special privilege and a sublime state, He bestows on that person all the gifts necessary for his state and adornment."

"Anne was the most chaste of virgins," wrote **Mary of Agreda** in *The Mystical City of God.* "From her very childhood, she possessed the fullness of every virtue. She was continually engaged in devout meditation. Her unceasing prayer was that the Redeemer might come soon."

As the works of God are perfect, it was natural to expect that He should make St. Anne a worthy mother of that most pure creature who was superior in sanctity to all creatures and inferior only to God. Had St. Anne not been adorned with angelic purity, she could not have become the mother of the Virgin of virgins. The great miracle of Mary's Immaculate Conception fittingly took place in St. Anne's pure womb.

In her visions, the servant of God, **Anne Catherine Emmerich**, beheld St. Anne in ecstasy, enveloped in heavenly splendor and surrounded by a host of Angels at the moment of Mary's Immaculate Conception. She beheld how the heavens opened, and she saw the holy Angels and the Most Holy Trinity rejoice. Equally great was the jubilation at the Blessed Virgin's birth. These are but a few rays of St. Anne's dignity and sanctity.

VENERATION OF ST. ANNE

How long has St. Anne been honored by Catholics? **Baronius**, a celebrated ecclesiastical writer, says: "Veneration of St. Anne is as ancient as the Church itself. In the East and in the West, she has been venerated from the beginning." It is related that the Apostles themselves transformed St. Anne's dwelling at Jerusalem into a church. Why is St. Anne one of the most popular Saints of Holy Church? Because of the plenitude of her virtues, the height of her exalted dignity and her close relationship with the holiest of all persons, Jesus and Mary.

After St. Joseph, no Saint enjoys such widespread veneration as good St. Anne. It would be impossible to enumerate the churches and chapels dedicated to her and the many places of pilgrimage where, in the course of centuries, manifold favors have been granted and astounding miracles wrought. The number of churches having an altar or image in honor of St. Anne is constantly increasing.

Love and veneration of the faithful for St. Anne is manifested in a practical way by giving the name "Anne" to girls in Baptism. Certainly, after the name of Mary, none is more beautiful. Frequently the two names, Mary and Anne, are combined.

MIRACULOUS DISCOVERY OF RELICS

According to a most ancient and uninterrupted tradition, the body of St. Anne was carried to Gaul* by the same vessel which carried Lazarus and his sisters there. During the first century of the Christian era, these friends of Our Lord were banished from Palestine because of their faith. From their hands St. Anne's precious remains were

---

*Gaul was a province of the Roman empire which included what are now the countries of France and upper Italy.

taken for safekeeping to the city of Apta Julia, which in our own times is the city of Apt, France. In those stormy days of persecution, it was necessary to hide the relics of the martyrs and Saints. Consequently, the body of St. Anne was buried in an underground church or crypt. The martyrology of Apt, one of the most ancient in existence, mentions this fact.

The first bishop of Apta Julia, **St. Auspicius**, who died before 118, took further precautions to guard this holy treasure from desecration and had the body buried still deeper in the subterranean chapel. All approach to it was carefully concealed till persecutions and invasions should have ceased. For centuries, the country was repeatedly overrun by hordes of barbarians, and it was only natural that during these agitated years the precise spot where St. Auspicius had carefully hidden his treasure became lost in obscurity.

After Charlemagne's decisive victory over the Saracens at the close of the eighth century, peace and security returned to Gaul. It was then that the people began to restore and rebuild the holy places destroyed or desecrated by the invaders. Priests and bishops of Apta Julia began to seek for the exact spot in the deep crypt where St. Auspicius had hidden and walled up the sarcophagus of St. Anne.

Charlemagne's first care on his arrival at Apt was to have the cathedral reconsecrated. This took place during the Easter solemnities, in the presence of an enormous crowd of nobles, clergy and people. But there was one cause of sadness amid all the rejoicing, namely, that every effort to find the remains of St. Anne had proved fruitless. A miracle, however, was to lead to the discovery of her resting place, as is related by **Charlemagne** in a letter to Pope Adrian I.

Among the young nobles who accompanied their parents on this occasion was John, a lad of fourteen, the son of Baron Casanova, deaf, dumb and blind from birth. People near the boy in the sanctuary remarked that during the services he was carried away by some overpowering emotion. With rapt and upturned face he seemed to be listening to voices from above. Presently, he moved toward the high altar, struck with his staff the steps leading up to it and made signs that they should dig there. His persistence caused considerable disturbance amid the solemn rites, but neither the clergy nor the royal guards could quiet or restrain the youth.

Charlemagne was deeply impressed. After Mass, he commanded that the excavation desired by the boy should be made. The altar steps were removed and a door, closed up with huge stones, was revealed. This was the door of the ancient crypt in which St. Auspicius had been accustomed to celebrate the holy Mysteries and to feed his flock with the Bread of Life. Its size and adornments reminded one of the Roman catacombs. No sooner had this door been opened and the flight of steps leading down from it disclosed than the blind boy rushed forward, as if his eyes had been suddenly opened, and led the way into this underground church. Charlemagne now held the boy's hand and gave orders to keep back the excited multitude.

John made signs that they should search farther, and he struck the wall of the crypt, indicating that what they sought lay beyond. When the wall was broken down, another and lower crypt was discovered at the end of a long and narrow corridor. As they came in view of this crypt, a bright light flashed upon the Emperor and his assistants. They beheld, in front of a walled recess, a burning lamp which flooded the place with unearthly splendor. No sooner, however, had the Emperor and his cortege entered this place, than the lamp went out. But, more wonderful still, at that very moment the blind boy could see, speak and hear. "The body of Saint Anne, mother of the Virgin Mary, Mother of God, is in yonder recess," were his first words.

The awe-stricken Emperor and his followers, at first dumb with amazement, gave vent to their emotion in words of praise and thanksgiving. The walled recess was thrown open, a sweet fragrance like that of oriental balm filled the air, and a casket of cypress wood was discovered containing the body of St. Anne wrapped round and round with folds of precious cloth. On the casket was the inscription: "Here lies the body of Blessed Anne, mother of the Virgin Mary."

Charlemagne, with all those present, venerated the sacred deposit thus brought to light. Afterward he had an exact narrative of the discovery drawn up by one of his notaries and a copy sent to the Pope with the royal letter. This letter and the Pope's answer are still extant.

The miraculous discovery at once made the Cathedral of Apt the center of attraction for Christian pilgrims from every part of Gaul. In the wars which followed the reign of Charlemagne down to our own times, the clergy and people of Apt have watched with never failing love over the sacred treasure which is the glory of their city. Travelers visiting the venerable Cathedral of St. Auspicius will find piles of ex votos, the indisputable testimonies during eleven centuries of the wonders wrought there by Christ at the intercession of His sainted Grandmother.

The chief cities of Gaul hastened to solicit from the church of Apta Julia portions of the hallowed body thus miraculously discovered. Fragments detached from the head found their way to various places through the favor of sovereigns or powerful prelates, but the greatest portion of St. Anne's sacred body still reposes in Apt.

Vienna, Austria, possesses the right hand of St. Anne, which is devoutly venerated in the beautiful church which bears her name.

An arm of the Saint was solicited and obtained by the Popes and placed under the care of the Benedictine monks in the magnificent monastery church of St. Paul-Outside-the-Walls in Rome. In May, 1960, the Benedictines gave the forearm to the Shrine of St. Anne de Beaupre in Canada.

In the Cathedral of Bologna, Italy, a large portion of the Saint's head is venerated.

Through these precious relics, which have proved efficacious in every kind of distress, miracles have been wrought—up to the present day.

VENERATION OF ST. ANNE IN THE AMERICAS

The Spanish missionaries in particular, who labored in Mexico and South America, sought to inspire their converts with affection for St. Anne.

These zealous heralds of the Faith, while announcing the doctrine of our Divine Saviour, also laid the foundation of fervent and tender devotion to Mary, His virgin Mother, and proclaimed everywhere the honor and glory of good St. Anne.

ST. ANNE DE BEAUPRÉ

In recent years, the New World has been venerating St. Anne in a special manner. Canada claims the title of the "Land of St. Anne." The early missionaries who came from Bretagne (Brittany), France, firmly established devotion to St. Anne in the hearts of the faithful. The first and principal place of pilgrimage to the honor of St. Anne in Canada was Beaupré, with its magnificent basilica of St. Anne.

The history of this shrine is as interesting as it is miraculous.

One night in 1650, some sailors were overtaken on the St. Lawrence by a frightful storm. Their vessel was driven by the wind and waves toward the rocky banks. They were seemingly about to perish, and no earthly aid was near. In their peril, they implored the help of good St. Anne, the patroness of their beloved Brittany, and vowed, if saved, to build a chapel in her honor on whatever spot they should land.

Morning dawned, and to their great astonishment, they found themselves on the north bank of the river at Beaupré. They landed and erected a little shrine in honor of good St. Anne, their deliverer. In 1656, Beaupré was made a parish by Msgr. de Laval, Bishop of Quebec. A parish church was erected the following year.

While the foundation of the building was being laid, the first attested marvel was wrought. Louis Guimond, a prey to keen sufferings, cherished an ardent devotion to St. Anne. He wished to have a share in erecting a shrine in her honor and managed to bring three stones for the foundation of the church. After accomplishing this act of devotion, he was suddenly and completely cured.

The wonders began to multiply. They were attested by **Bishop de Laval** in 1662. **Father Morel**, who was pastor at that time, wrote: "Of much more importance than all these cures are the spiritual graces daily bestowed by Almighty God through the intercession of good St. Anne on many a sinner, by converting him to a better life. Having performed the pastoral functions in the church for five or six years, I have known many persons who experienced the grace of so happy a change."

In 1662, while Father Morel was still pastor at Beaupré, **Blessed Marie of the Incarnation**, who was the foundress of the Ursuline Nuns of Quebec, wrote from that city to a relative who lived back in France:

"Some twenty miles from here . . . is a church of St. Anne in which Our Lord works great wonders for the sake of the holy mother of the most Blessed Virgin Mary. At this shrine, paralytics obtain strength to walk, the blind receive their sight, and the sick, no matter what their ailment may be, regain their health."

Nearly three centuries have elapsed since then, but the wonders wrought by good St. Anne have never ceased. In time a basilica, magnificent in its beauty and proportions, was erected to her honor at Beaupré. Its most remarkable feature was the countless number of crutches, canes, trusses and even eyeglasses which were suspended or piled in the chapels as the *ex votos* of innumerable invalids who thus bore witness to their recovery through the assistance of good St. Anne.

DESTRUCTION AND REBUILDING

But even such monuments are in the hands of Divine Providence, and as though to indicate that a yet worthier monument should be dedicated to the honor of good St. Anne, the magnificent basilica was completely destroyed by fire on the morning of March 29, 1922. After the hungry flames had completed their work of destruction, all that remained of the splendid structure were broken and scattered turrets, charred and dismantled walls, heaps of debris, seared and scattered *ex votos*. The disaster was complete, but wonder of wonders, over the shapeless mass of what had been the basilica, above the crumbling portal, between the two broken towers, stood the wooden statue of St. Anne, holding in her arms the Blessed Virgin Mary. And standing unscathed amid the ruins, the miraculous statue of the Saint still held in its gilt casing the great relic of St. Anne.

What was to be done to accommodate the crowds of pilgrims who came to venerate the wondrous statue? The problem was solved by erecting a temporary church. In thirty-seven days St. Anne was provided with a new "basilica," a simple wooden church in which the miraculous statue was enshrined and which witnessed the cures of thousands of devout clients. But alas, during the night of November 8, 1926, the wooden framework of this temporary basilica fell prey to another conflagration.

Rising upon the ashes of this modest shrine to the honor of St. Anne is the present great Basilica, beautiful and majestic in its Romanesque architecture, indeed a worthy monument in stone to the great Saint from whose maternal heart streams of mercy have flowed to mankind.

Well over two million pilgrims visit the shrine annually, proving how greatly St. Anne is venerated among the faithful and what confidence they place in her intercession. Since the beginning of the shrine in 1658, over 46,500,000 pilgrims and visitors from all over the world have come to venerate the relics of good St. Anne and to implore her intercession. The peak of 2,000,000 visitors was reached in 1957. Many people come in pilgrimages, which are becoming ever more popular. St. Anne's feast (July 26) always draws immense crowds to the shrine. As is natural, most of the visitors are from the United States and Canada, though far distant parts of the globe are not without representatives.*

The year 1958 marked the Third Centenary of the founding of the Shrine of St. Anne de Beaupré. Nearly three million pilgrims took part in the Tercentennial celebrations, inaugurated on the first Sunday of May and concluded on October 12. Congresses, pilgrimages, novenas, triduums and symposia highlighted each month.

---

*Note: All information in this booklet regarding numbers of visitors and sizes of crowds is from the 1963 edition. —*Publisher*, 1998.

PRECIOUS RELICS

The Church of St. Anne de Beaupré in Quebec, Canada has long been privileged to possess a rare relic of the Saint. It is a fragment of the wrist bone of St. Anne, about two or three inches in length, with the skin and flesh still adhering to the bone and showing the joint near the thumb. When the precious relic arrived in New York from Rome on May 1, 1892, a holy enthusiasm seized the busy metropolis. Crowds of the faithful began to flock to the church of St. Jean Baptiste, where the relic was temporarily deposited for the veneration of the faithful. It was a spectacle never before witnessed in the New World.

After obtaining this relic, the Redemptorist Fathers, guardians of the Shrine of St. Anne de Beaupré, sought to obtain possession of the forearm from which the wrist bone had been detached in 1892. This relic had been venerated for centuries in the Major Basilica of St. Paul-Outside-the-Walls in Rome. In May, 1960, this cherished desire of the Redemptorist Fathers was realized when the Benedictines in charge of the Basilica of St. Paul donated the entire forearm of St. Anne to the Basilica of St. Anne de Beaupré. This relic measures seven inches in length by two inches at the base.

On the occasion of its translation, splendid spiritual celebrations again took place in the church of St. Jean Baptiste in New York and at the Shrine of St. Anne de Beaupré. On July 3, 1960, the first Sunday of the month of St. Anne, the new relic was solemnly enthroned in the Basilica of St. Anne, where it has since been venerated by the crowds of pilgrims who come to the shrine.

ST. ANNE OF NEW YORK

So great had been the enthusiasm of the faithful of New York in venerating the relic of St. Anne in 1892, when on its way to the Shrine of St. Anne de Beaupré, that it had remained exposed for three weeks, instead of three days, as first intended. Throngs gathered from every direction. Their pious zeal was rewarded by Pope Leo XIII, who soon afterward presented them with a considerable portion of the forearm of St. Anne, which since that time has been preserved and devoutly venerated in the church of St. Jean Baptiste.

In October, 1900, the Fathers of the Blessed Sacrament, whose chief work is the perpetual adoration of the Blessed Sacrament, were put in charge of the church. Such numbers of worshipers came to honor the Blessed Sacrament and St. Anne that the church proved too small. In 1901 a crypt dedicated to St. Anne was built under the upper church, but this too soon proved inadequate. However, on the appeal of Cardinal Farley, generous donations of the devotees of the Blessed Sacrament and St. Anne made it possible to erect a magnificent new church, at 194 E. 76th St. (Lexington Avenue and East 76th Street), which was opened in February, 1913.

St. Anne, as if to show her gratitude, has not ceased to bestow marvelous cures and spiritual and temporal favors upon her children. In the sanctuary, tier upon tier of crutches, canes and braces witness her miraculous power. Four times daily the relic is applied to the sick, the lame, the blind, the broken-hearted and the needy. Every Tuesday,* the perpetual novena services are attended by large crowds.

Every year, solemn novena services are held before the feast of St. Anne in July, and large as the church is, the novena crowds strain its capacity to the utmost. Nine Masses are celebrated daily, and thousands of Holy Communions are

---

*While we have checked all the U.S. shrines mentioned in this booklet to make sure they still exist, anyone who wishes to attend devotions at any of them is advised to call beforehand to check the schedule. Also, those shrines which are not located inside a parish church may not be open every day.—*Publisher*, 1998.

distributed during the novena. Seven priests are on duty in the confessionals from early morning until night. Two sermons and Benediction of the Blessed Sacrament are given in the afternoon and evening; the holy relic is applied almost continuously from morning until late at night. Conservative estimates put the number of pilgrims who visit the shrine during the novena at no less than 100,000.

OTHER SHRINES OF ST. ANNE IN THE UNITED STATES

While the other shrines of St. Anne in the United States are not so widely known as that in New York and that of St. Anne de Beaupré in Canada, nevertheless the Saint does not disdain to work the prodigies of her goodness elsewhere too.

The Blessed Sacrament Fathers and Brothers have a shrine to St. Anne in Cleveland at 5384 Wilson Mills Rd. St. Anne's shrine stands next to St. Paschal's Church.

In Arvada, Colorado (7555 Grant Place), there is a shrine dedicated to St. Anne which is privileged to possess a true relic of the Saint, a particle of bone. In former years the relic was venerated publicly every Thursday evening, at which time a perpetual novena was conducted. Many graces and favors were received there yearly through the intercession of good St. Anne.

In the Middle West, also, are located several shrines of St. Anne, the one in Chicago, Illinois being known as "St. Anne of Brighton Park." This shrine was begun in 1900 by French Canadians. Its simple origin centered about the authentic relics of the Saint, portions of bones, the largest being about one inch in length. Because of the many reported miracles and spiritual favors received, the shrine grew to be one of the largest and most notable in the United States and has attracted thousands of pilgrims who are unable to journey to the more famous shrine of St. Anne de Beaupré. At the Fountain of St. Anne, the waters of which pass over the encased relic of the saint, many cures have been wrought, and there are on record at the shrine the names of hundreds of persons who have been cured or helped by the holy mother of the Blessed Virgin.

The shrine itself is a chapel in Our Lady of Fatima parish at West 38th Place (formerly the church of St. Joseph and St. Anne at 3836 S. California Avenue). Devotions to St. Anne are held there every Thursday.

The Basilica of St. Mary in Minneapolis, Minnesota, was formerly a center of devotion to St. Anne and is still blessed in the possession of a precious relic of the Saint, which is now imbedded in a side altar. In former years the devoted clients of St. Anne came in large numbers to venerate the relic when it was presented for public veneration, and many favors were received through the loving mother of the Mother of Mercy. (In recent years the shrine of St. Anne has also served as a memorial to children and youths who have died.)

A fitting monument to the glories of St. Anne is the shrine in Scranton, Pennsylvania, known as St. Anne of Scranton, or St. Anne's Basilica parish. It is located at 1239 St. Anne St. and is served by the Passionist Fathers. A perpetual novena is conducted there every Monday, and a steady stream of clients continues from early morning till night. For centuries St. Anne has been invoked as patroness of miners, and it surely cannot be a coincidence that this shrine is located in the center of the anthracite coal mining region.

In St. Louis, Missouri, too, there is a shrine to St. Anne. It is now a combined parish called Visitation-St. Anne's Shrine. The parish is listed in the *Catholic Directory* as "African-American." The church is located at 4145 Evans Ave. Devotions are held every Thursday.

In the village of St. Anne, Illinois, a novena of Masses is held yearly at St. Anne Catholic Church from July 18 to July 26, with other festive observances on July 26, the Feast of St. Anne. St. Anne Church was founded in 1872; it is blessed to possess a relic of the Saint. The church is located about 60 miles south of Chicago and 15 miles southeast of Kankakee. The novena has been the occasion of many blessings, both spiritual and physical—as testified by the canes, crutches and wheelchairs left behind.

In the south, New Orleans, Louisiana, boasts of a beautiful shrine of St. Anne, dedicated in 1935. It consists of a grotto and small gift shop located at 2101 Ursuline Avenue (Ursuline and Johnston), next to St. Peter Claver Parish (with which it is not connected). Although Church authorities had decided in 1995 to close the shrine, they consented to allow lay devotees of St. Anne to keep it open on a limited basis. Currently the shrine is open a few mornings per week (Tuesdays, Saturdays and Sundays—and Fridays in Lent).

While the above-mentioned shrine is the original shrine of St. Anne in New Orleans, the title of

National Shrine of St. Anne now belongs to St. Anne Church and Shrine, located at 3601 Transcontinental in nearby Metairie, Louisiana 70006. Devotions are held there on Tuesday nights. The St. Anne Group of New Orleans, which had taken over the work of constructing a basilica and other units, was raised to the rank of an Archconfraternity for the whole United States by Pius XI on May 18, 1926.

A relic of St. Anne is venerated in the relic chapel of St. Mary's College in St. Mary's, Kansas.

The Benedictine Sisters of Clyde, Missouri are privileged to possess a small particle of bone of St. Anne, which is enshrined in their relic chapel. Visitors are welcome to visit the chapel. The convent and chapel are located on County Road P, off Hwy 136, 16 miles SSE of Maryville.

THE BLESSED VIRGIN MARY AND ST. ANNE

Veneration of St. Anne is closely allied to veneration of the Blessed Virgin Mary. The feasts of Mary's nativity and presentation are in reality feasts of St. Anne, as all praises referring to the daughter are directed also to the mother. Mary surpasses all the faithful in veneration, esteem and in tender and filial love for her holy mother. While Anne and Mary lived on earth, the bond of love that united their hearts was most ardent and intimate. Nor has this bond been dissolved in Heaven. Rather, it has been drawn still closer and has become indissoluble for all eternity.

Mary once appeared to one of her clients and asked her to add to her customary Rosary devotion an *Our Father* and *Hail Mary* in honor of Mary's holy mother, St. Anne. "Those who honor

A replica of the beautiful statue of St. Anne with the child Mary (modeled on the painting of the famous artist Franz Ittenbach) venerated in the relic chapel of the Benedictine Sisters at Clyde, Missouri.

St. Anne," said Our Lady, "will obtain great aid in every need, especially at the hour of death." To another person she said: "The honor you show to my mother is doubly dear and pleasing to me."

The learned Bollandists relate that a hermit who was especially devoted to the Blessed Virgin was once seized with bitter anguish of spirit. He fled for refuge to the Queen of Heaven. Radiant with splendor, Mary appeared to him and said: "Since you are lovingly devoted to me, I will take away all your grief and sorrow of soul, but I admonish you to venerate and praise my dear mother also, if you desire great graces from me. I am highly pleased with the affection accorded to my beloved mother. Know, too, that my Son, Jesus, has promised to deliver from misfortune all who honor my mother and to assist them in attaining eternal glory. My son, practice this devotion and make it known."

After speaking these words, Mary vanished, leaving a heavenly perfume in the hermit's cell. The anchorite faithfully complied with the request of the Virgin Mother. From that time on, to every greeting addressed to the Queen of Heaven, he added the prayer: "And blessed be thy sweet mother, Anne, from whom thou didst assume thy virginal flesh."

If we wish to give Mary special joy, let us

fervently venerate St. Anne, for every child is pleased to see her mother honored.

HOW THE SAINTS HONORED ST. ANNE

It would be impossible to enumerate the many Saints who practiced great devotion to St. Anne. **St. Augustine**, the illustrious Doctor who illumined the Church of God with his profound wisdom, practiced an ardent devotion to St. Anne. Every year on the Saint's feast, he preached on her virtues and dignity with an eloquence which encouraged and inspired his numerous hearers.

St. John Damascene, another Doctor of the Church, not only most ardently venerated Mary, but St. Anne as well. He preached many sermons in her honor and composed books that treated of her glory and dignity. "St. Anne," he declares in his writing, "is a generous mother, a compassionate mother, a gracious mother, because the word 'Anne' means 'generous, merciful, gracious.'"

St. Thomas Aquinas, hailed as one of the greatest of intellectuals, a prodigy of learning, a pillar of Holy Church, an angel of wisdom and one of the most eminent Doctors of the Church, was a fervent client of good St. Anne. His example ought to strengthen our confidence in this privileged Saint and urge us to venerate her most fervently. He frequently refers to St. Anne and sets forth reasons for honoring her dignity and power. He assures us that the privilege of aiding man in every distress has been given to good St. Anne.

St. Teresa of Avila, the seraphic virgin and reformer of religious discipline, entertained a tender love of St. Anne. This highly gifted teacher of prayer delighted to speak of St. Anne's dignity and power, and she inspired those under her care with a fervent affection for Our Lady's mother. In all convents of the Carmelite Order, she introduced special devotions to St. Anne. The same was done by **St. Bridget** in her order.

Anne Catherine Emmerich, who bore the sacred stigmata in her body, said, "In desperate cases of need, I always invoke the holy mother Anne."

POWER OF ST. ANNE'S INTERCESSION

Almighty God privileged St. Anne above all others in choosing her to be the mother of the Queen of Heaven. This favored Saint ranks high in merit and glory, near to the Word Incarnate and to His most holy Mother. Certainly, then, St. Anne has great power with God. Yes, assuredly the mother of the most powerful and amiable Virgin is likewise full of power and mercy.

To many Saints God has granted the power of working miracles. He told His Apostles that they would do greater things than He had done. Now surely, what He promised to His chosen followers He would not refuse to His own grandmother! Those related to Him by the ties of blood were dear to Him in life and still have great power through their intercession. There can be no question, then, that St. Anne has great influence over her Divine Grandson and that by her intercessory power she can also work miracles in favor of her clients.

Tradition, the history of the Church and the chronicles of various places of pilgrimage have recorded countless miracles wrought by Christ through the intercession of His sainted grandmother. Nor have they ceased to this day. Yearly, hundreds of thousands of persons visit the shrine of St. Anne de Beaupré in Canada alone. Many are cured of diseases; all are comforted and consoled. These favors serve to strengthen and confirm our trust and confidence in the power of the intercession of good St. Anne.

The famous and learned **Abbot Trithemius** practiced an extraordinary devotion to St. Anne and did all in his power to induce others to venerate her. He wrote a book in her praise in which he says: "To St. Anne God has given the power to aid in every necessity, because Jesus, her Divine Grandchild according to the flesh, will refuse her no petition, and Mary, her glorious daughter, supports her every request. Those who venerate good St. Anne shall want for nothing, either in this life or the next. Believe me, if you love and venerate this Saint, you will experience how highly God esteems her. He grants all she asks! It would be impossible to enumerate the many graces she obtains daily for her servants."

The same writer continues: "St. Anne by her intercession dispels melancholy and evil desires. She also aids the poor, cures the sick and comforts the sorrowing. She removes tribulations and by her intercession obtains for her clients the grace to eradicate vice and implant virtue. She obtains light for the intellect, strength for the will and affection for the heart. This powerful Saint has preserved thousands from contagious diseases. Through her intercession, evil spirits have been expelled. For the barren in the married state, she obtains children and heavenly assistance in delivery. She inspires the despairing with trust in God's mercy and excites the tepid to zeal and fervor. St. Anne has rescued many from imminent death; yes, through her intercession the dead have, in several instances, been restored to life. Those who worthily venerate St. Anne can obtain aid in every necessity through her mediation."

Pope Gregory XIII, when introducing the feast of St. Anne into the Church, declared: "We believe that St. Anne continually intercedes for us with the merciful Lord, for through her great benefits have come to mankind. From her was born the ever pure and immaculate Virgin Mary, who was found worthy to bring forth Jesus Christ, our Redeemer."

Pope Gregory XV encourages us thus: "We do not doubt that the more love we show to the mother of Mary, the more we merit the intercession and aid of the holy Virgin who brought forth the only-begotten Son of God, Our Lord Jesus Christ."

St. Teresa of Avila often said: "We know and are convinced that our good mother St. Anne helps in all needs, dangers and tribulations, for Our Lord wishes to show us that He will do also in Heaven what she asks of Him for us."

The saintly **Abbot Trithemius** again exhorts us: "Approach St. Anne, your amiable protectress, with full confidence. Knock at her gates with persevering prayer, because she can obtain for you the forgiveness of your sins and can open Heaven for you. She lacks nothing that can profit you. . . . Believe me, who have already obtained many a favor through her whom the Queen of Heaven honors as her dearest mother. . . . No one knows, no one believes, how many favors God confers on lovers of St. Anne!"

PATRONESS OF CHRISTIAN MOTHERS

St. Anne is the great model of all in the married state and of those otherwise charged with the education of children. Great was her honor in being the mother of the Mother of God and in giving to a lost world the Advocate of Mercy. Sublime was her office in instructing this blessed child in virtue and holiness.

St. Anne herself was a "vessel of grace," not in name only, but in the possession of those gifts with which God had endowed her to be the worthy mother of the Virgin Mary. Her motherly care for the Blessed Virgin was the means of St. Anne's sanctification. Because of this she receives and will receive a special glory in the Church to the end of ages.

How encouraging this is to all parents who make the holy education of their children their principal duty. By this they glorify their Creator, perpetuate His honor on earth and sanctify their own souls. From the hands of the parents God will one day require the souls of their children. Happy will those parents be who can say to the Divine Judge: "Not one of those whom Thou hast given me has been lost through my fault."

Realizing, therefore, the great duty she has in rearing her children well, the Catholic mother will daily recommend her children to God and pray especially to St. Anne for the gift of imparting to them a good training, the highest and most difficult of all arts.

St. Anne obtains many graces, priceless graces, for all who venerate her, but she grants her maternal assistance in particular to Christian mothers who choose her for their patroness and model. Numberless examples prove that St. Anne obtains great favors for Christian mothers. She preserves peace in married life, restores harmony in discord and often wonderfully changes the bad disposition of a husband or wife. She protects the birth of children in an extraordinary manner; bestows blessings that lighten the task of rearing children properly; brings wayward children back upon the right path; obtains restoration to health for the mother when sick; preserves her precious life for her family, for her helpless children; and prevents the loss of husband and father. She revealed to St. Bridget that she would protect all who live chastely and peacefully in the married state.

St. Anne is glorious among the Saints, not only because she is the mother of Mary, but also because she gave Mary to God. She did not hesitate to sacrifice this child, her greatest joy, to the call of God, dedicating her at the age of three to His service in the Temple. In this she is a beautiful example to parents to foster and encourage vocations to the religious life among their children, rather than running the dread risk of hindering them. Through the intercession of St. Anne, parents come to know and acknowledge divine guidance and learn that children are born to them not for earthly ends, but for God.

TITLES OF ST. ANNE

In the glorious Middle Ages, St. Anne was fondly called:

Comfortress of the Sorrowing—Mother of the Poor—Health of the Sick—Patroness of the Childless—Help of the Pregnant—Model of

Married Women and Mothers—Protectress of Widows—Patroness of Laborers.

Comfortress of the Sorrowing. St. Anne was spared neither trials nor bitterness. God tested her severely, especially by ordaining that she would have to wait so long for Mary, her child of predilection. For years, hidden sorrow was her daily bread.

Mother of the Poor. St. Anne's love for the poor is evident from the praise bestowed upon her by St. John Damascene, who relates that she and St. Joachim distributed one third of their possessions to the poor. St. Anne still continues her charity in Heaven by assisting the poor, often in a wonderful manner. Nor does St. Anne forget the dying, the poorest of the poor. These, above all others, experience her motherly protection.

Health of the Sick. The number of cures wrought through the intercession of St. Anne is countless. Day after day the churches dedicated to her, as that at St. Anne de Beaupré, have resounded with the suppliant voices of her clients. Sight has been restored to the blind, hearing to the deaf, soundness to the bodies of the infirm and crippled.

These are the exterior signs of the power and maternal goodness of St. Anne, but what shall we say of the interior cures of spiritual ailments known to God alone? How many times has the good Saint strengthened a wavering courage, given a new vitality to a languid spiritual life, opened a mind to the light of the true Faith? Numberless prodigies of this kind have taken place at the Shrine of St. Anne, unknown to men for the most part, but known to God, whose loving Providence seems to take delight in granting multiplied graces through the intercession of good St. Anne, so that the *ex votos*, the mute testimonies of innumerable physical cures, could well be supplemented by testimonials of spiritual favors, were such a thing possible.

Good St. Anne, like a true and faithful mother, does not turn a deaf ear to the pleas of her children; and as a mother's heart is deeply touched at the sight of the afflictions of her children, so is St. Anne's motherly heart touched by the petitions of those who come to her seeking solace and comfort.

Patroness of the Childless. Childless mothers invoke good St. Anne because, only after many years of married life, did this Saint finally receive from God the child of grace, Mary. Full of compassion for those in like sorrow, she intercedes with God and, if it be His holy will, obtains for them the favor which completes the happiness of conjugal union.

Help of the Pregnant. This office of good St. Anne is connected with the foregoing. As she obtains for women the much-desired favor of motherhood, so she will also guard the fruit of the womb, so that the child may receive holy Baptism. She assists mothers when they are in their great anxiety, and she obtains a happy delivery.

Model of Married Women and Mothers. St. Anne is the shining example of all Christian women. This was her vocation on earth as wife of St. Joachim and mother of the Blessed Virgin. She is, indeed, the patroness of Christian women and mothers, their special protectress and advocate, having herself borne the heavy burdens of the married state and tasted all the bitterness which makes this vocation difficult. In every family where good St. Anne is invoked, she shows herself a loving protectress, and never has she been venerated or invoked in vain.

She obtains for women, particularly in our misguided age, the light to understand the high purpose of Matrimony. God instituted this Sacrament for the propagation of mankind. Since the Fall, the state of Matrimony is, especially for the wife, a state of penance, of labor, of submission. But although children are often a source of much trouble and care to parents, particularly to the mother, they are, nevertheless, to be regarded as a blessing, "the blessing of children," for they are a gift of God, a pledge of His fatherly goodness. This is the sublime, the sacred purpose of Matrimony: to bring forth children who will be children of God, heirs of Heaven, who are destined to possess forever the places of the Fallen Angels! The hope of the Church is in good Christian mothers; their sons and daughters will fill the sanctuaries and convents.

Protectress of Widows. Difficult is the state of the Christian widow. Bereft of her husband, her staff and the support of her children, she stands alone in the world—if poor, doubly needy. Is it any wonder, then, that Holy Scripture, after recommending to our charity the poor and orphans, also begs our compassion for widows? Their patroness, good St. Anne, will lovingly shield and protect them in their many dangers and temptations, both spiritual and temporal. Hence, Christian widows feel drawn to place themselves under her powerful protection.

Patroness of Laborers. Among the various classes of laborers, many regard St. Anne as their special protectress. But it is very significant that Christian sculptors venerate her as their model. They have chosen as their emblem the image of St. Anne teaching the child Mary, with these words inscribed beneath: "Thus she wrought the Tabernacle of God." For every Christian sculptor, the Tabernacle, the dwelling of God, is in a certain sense the masterpiece of his art.

ST. ANNE OBTAINS FOR HER CLIENTS A HAPPY DEATH

As the Blessed Virgin revealed, St. Anne obtains for her clients the grace of a happy death. A priest tells of this experience of St. Anne's power:

"While I was assistant pastor in the parish of X, I was aroused one night by the ringing of the door bell. A stately woman, a stranger to me, called up the stairs: 'Father, please go quickly and take the Blessed Sacrament to a servant in a house upon the hill, for she will not live through the night. The sexton is waiting for you in the church.'

"The sexton had been awakened by the same person. I took the Blessed Sacrament, and we started for the house. An hour later we arrived. To our great surprise, we found the house locked, and nowhere a sound or a light. We knocked at the door, but when it was opened, no one knew anything of a servant being ill there, so we concluded that some person, wishing to make light of us, had deceived us. However, in order that I would not need to return with the Blessed Sacrament, one of the servants declared her readiness to go to Confession and to receive Holy Communion. Her suggestion was readily accepted. During her Confession, she began to feel indisposed. She finished her Confession and received Holy Communion. Before long her condition became worse, and she was obliged to go to bed. Soon it was evident that her end was near. I administered Extreme Unction and imparted the indulgence for the dying. Scarcely had this been done when the servant died.

"About her bed hung pictures of many Saints, among which was a large decorated representation of St. Anne. 'This servant,' said the inmates of the house, 'practiced special devotion to St. Anne. In her honor she abstained from milk every Tuesday.' I have no doubt that the woman who called the sexton and myself was none other than St. Anne, who obtained for her client this last great favor."

Let us practice special devotion to St. Anne in

order to obtain a happy death, upon which depends our happiness for all eternity.

TUESDAY DEDICATED TO ST. ANNE

St. Anne obtains numerous favors for those who dedicate Tuesday to her honor. The Blessed Virgin is said to have revealed to different Saints that she wished them to practice special devotion in honor of her glorious mother each Tuesday.

An ancient tradition tells us that when St. Anne was about to die, Our Lord addressed her thus:

"Blessed art thou, My beloved grand-parent! All who venerate thee shall have blessings for soul and body. If they invoke thee in their needs, I will hear them for thy name's sake. Since thou dost die on a Tuesday, I appoint this day for thy honor, and I will grant the prayers of all who honor thee on this day."

Various devotions may be practiced on Tuesdays. It will greatly please St. Anne if on this day we assist at Holy Mass and receive Holy Communion in her honor and offer it to God in thanksgiving for the prerogatives bestowed upon her. St. Gertrude beheld in a vision how pleasing it is to the Saints if we thank God for the graces He has bestowed upon them. It was revealed to her that those who do this will be adorned with the merits of the Saints they thus honor.

There is also another simple way by which we may show our veneration for St. Anne. We are told that she was very charitable and gave alms freely. It will give her great joy if we give alms in her honor on Tuesdays.

One may also pray the *Hail Mary* nine times in honor of the nine months during which she bore the Immaculate Virgin Mary in her womb. Clients of St. Anne should devoutly celebrate her feast day, July 26, and prepare for it by a novena (a prayer said for nine days). Lastly, we should try to spread devotion to good St. Anne, which can be done effectively by circulating this booklet.

CURED BY ST. ANNE

In 1917, Miss Kirby of Newark, New Jersey, experienced a severe pain in her hip. The doctor ordered her not to use her foot for six weeks. At St. Joseph's Hospital in Paterson, New Jersey, three X-rays were taken and a brace made for the foot. Miss Kirby wore the brace, though it occasioned her intense pain and caused sores to form on her foot. She went to several other doctors and had eight more X-rays taken, but treatments were of no avail. Some doctors declared it to be tuberculosis, others a hip disease.

Concerning her cure in 1920, we quote her own words: "I had heard a great deal of St. Anne's devotion, and the Sisters of St. Joseph where I attended school told me of the relic of St. Anne. This filled me with great faith and confidence in St. Anne. My mother was going to take me to another doctor, but I asked her to take me to the church, where I had the relic applied to my foot, and within one hour I had a complete cure. At once I bought a statue of St. Anne and had a Mass said in her honor. I promised to return to the same church for a few Sundays, to do all in my power to spread devotion to St. Anne and to spend one hour a week in the presence of the Blessed Sacrament in thanksgiving for the great favor which I feel St. Anne granted me. Thanks to God and dear St. Anne!"

ANOTHER PRODIGY

The following account is taken from the *Annals of Good Saint Anne de Beaupré* of August, 1937:

"St. Paul, Minn., May 12, 1937

"About four years ago my son, then twenty-two

years old, was flying in an airplane with a friend when their plane crashed and landed in water. Coming down, the plane hit some electric power lines, but through a miracle of God, my son was saved from being burned to death. The accident, however, left him in such a state that no one thought he would reach the hospital alive. I happened to be some fifty miles from the town. When they notified me of the accident, the first thing I thought of was prayer, and I pleaded that my son would live until I reached the hospital. When I arrived, the nurse took me into the room, and I did not know my own son, for there was not a bone in his face that was not smashed, and his head was about three times its normal size. The doctors were doing all they could, but they saw very little hope of recovery.

"I at once implored the help of good St. Anne, who had never failed me, and I begged her to ask the Lord to save my son, to preserve him from being blind or crippled. I promised to send her the only thing of value I had, a gold watch, that it might be used for the altar or some such purpose. I stayed beside my son all day and all night, as they thought the end would come at any time. Toward morning he spoke, telling me not to worry, as he felt he was going to be all right. In one week's time, my boy walked out of the hospital with me. When people saw him, they could not believe their eyes.

"After taking treatments for a year (for the accident had left a hole in the roof of his mouth, which made it difficult for him to eat or drink), he was feeling much better. Now the doctors have put a silver plate in his mouth and he is back at work again. I wish to thank good St. Anne not only for this, but for the many other favors she has granted me."

—Mrs. J.L.

OTHER FAVORS

"In order to cure an insidious lung infection, two serious operations had to be performed on me. I prayed to St. Anne and the Blessed Mother to carry me through this ordeal safely. Thanks to them, I am well on the road to recovery."

—H.K., N.Y.

"It is with a grateful heart that I thank good St. Anne, who, through her powerful intercession with her divine Grandson and her beloved Daughter, has obtained my brother's return to the Sacraments after years of neglect. After twenty years he was reconciled to God on his deathbed and died a truly repentant death. His mind was crystal clear at the time of his reconciliation; his thoughts were continually on Heaven, and he repeatedly asked pardon for his sins. This happy death was little short of a miracle, as he had been very bitter against the Church. St. Anne is truly the Saint of Miracles. For years I prayed to her with confidence that my brother might see the error of his ways, and she has rewarded my trust."

—Ireland, June, 1962

"St. Anne has helped me through many heartaches and has been with me through the years. Many years ago, I made a novena to St. Anne for a special favor, promising to name my first child in her honor. My little girl is now three years old, and her name is Anne. St. Anne has also helped me to overcome a nervous breakdown. I only wish more people would pray to this wonderful Saint!"

—Mrs. E.U., New Jersey

"For sixteen years my mother suffered from acute rheumatic arthritis, which steadily grew worse. For the past six months she was unable to kneel and had the greatest difficulty in walking even a short distance. We had to help her in and out of her chair. We made several novenas to St. Anne for this intention and applied St. Anne's oil to the affected parts while praying for God's will to be done. Last night, for the first time in six months, she was able to kneel down without any help. I thank St. Anne from the bottom of my heart for this and countless other favors, particularly that of sending me a wonderful friend, who has brought me closer to Jesus and to her."

—Miss K.D., 1961

A CONSTANT FLOW OF TESTIMONIES

Each month the *Annals of Good St. Anne*, published at the shrine of St. Anne de Beaupré, Quebec, carries testimonials of marvelous favors obtained through the intercession of this good mother, which proves that her maternal solicitude extends to all times, to all needs.

The almost unceasing stream of pilgrimages to the shrine speaks louder than words concerning the faith and confidence which the faithful cherish in St. Anne's intercession. Truly impressive and inspiring is the devotion of the pilgrims here and at other shrines of this Saint.

ARCHCONFRATERNITY OF ST. ANNE

The Archconfraternity of St. Anne de Beaupré, erected in the Basilica of St. Anne de Beaupré, Quebec, Canada, on April 26, 1887, has since made gigantic progress and has been enriched with many indulgences.

Its object is to glorify St. Anne by rendering her veneration more universal and more practical; to extend to a greater number of souls those marvelous graces God has been pleased to bestow on her devout clients; to procure for the faithful, and more especially for poor sinners, for the sick, infirm and dying, the precious privilege of sharing in the immense union of prayers to St. Anne and in the Masses offered in her honor; to promote better Christian living.

In order to become a member of the Archconfraternity it is only necessary to be enrolled in the register of members, either at St. Anne de Beaupré or in any church in which the association may have been erected. If possible, personal presence is desirable, but in case of impossibility, registration may be made by letter.

Full information regarding pious practices observed by members, indulgences to be gained, etc. can be obtained from the Archconfraternity located at:

Shrine of St. Anne de Beaupré
10018 Royale Ave.
St. Anne de Beaupré, P.Q. G0A 3C0
CANADA

Prayers in Honor of St. Anne

MASS OF ST. ANNE
Feast, July 26

Proper of the Mass. May be used with a traditional prayer book containing the Ordinary of the Mass.

Introit. Let us all rejoice in the Lord, celebrating a festival day in honor of blessed Anne, on whose solemnity the Angels rejoice and give praise to the Son of God. *Ps*. 44. My heart hath uttered a good word: I speak my works to the King. *V.* Glory be to the Father . . .

Collect. O God, Who didst vouchsafe to endow blessed Anne with such grace that she was found worthy to be the mother of her who brought forth Thine only-begotten Son: grant, in Thy mercy, that we who keep her festival may be aided by her intercession with Thee. Through the same Lord Jesus Christ, Thy Son, who liveth and reigneth with Thee in the unity of the Holy Ghost, one God, world without end. Amen.

Epistle. (*Prov.* 31:10-31). Who shall find a valiant woman? Far and from the uttermost coasts is the price of her. The heart of her husband trusteth in her, and he shall have no need of spoils. She will render him good, and not evil, all the days of her life. . . . She hath opened her mouth to wisdom, and the law of clemency is on her tongue. She hath looked well to the paths of her house, and hath not eaten her bread idle. Her children rose up, and called her blessed: her husband, and he praised her. Many daughters have gathered together riches: thou hast surpassed them all. Favor is deceitful, and beauty is vain: the woman that feareth the Lord, she shall be praised. Give her of the fruit of her hands: and let her works praise her in the gates.

Gradual. *Ps.* 44. Thou hast loved justice and hated iniquity. *V.* Therefore God, thy God, hath anointed thee with the oil of gladness.

Alleluia. Alleluia, alleluia. *V.* Grace is poured abroad in thy lips: therefore hath God blessed thee forever and ever. Alleluia.

Gospel. (*Matt.* 13:44-52). At that time, Jesus spoke to His disciples this parable: "The kingdom of heaven is like unto a treasure hidden in a field.

Which a man having found, hid it, and for joy thereof goeth and selleth all that he hath, and buyeth that field. Again the kingdom of heaven is like to a merchant seeking good pearls. Who, when he had found one pearl of great price, went his way, and sold all that he had, and bought it. Again the kingdom of heaven is like to a net cast into the sea, and gathering together of all kind of fishes. Which, when it was filled, they drew out, and sitting by the shore, they chose out the good into vessels, but the bad they cast forth. So shall it be at the end of the world: the angels shall go out, and shall separate the wicked from among the just, and shall cast them into the furnace of fire: there shall be weeping and gnashing of teeth. Have ye understood all these things?" They say to him: "Yes." He said unto them: "Therefore every scribe instructed in the kingdom of heaven is like to a man that is a householder, who bringeth forth out of his treasure new things and old."

Offertory. *Ps.* 44:10. The daughters of kings have delighted thee in thy glory; the queen stood on thy right hand in gilded clothing, surrounded with variety.

Secret. Graciously regard, O Lord, we beseech Thee, these present sacrifices; that through the intercession of blessed Anne, who gave birth to the Mother of Thy Son, Our Lord Jesus Christ, they may increase our devotion and further our salvation. Through the same Lord Jesus Christ, Thy Son, who liveth and reigneth with Thee in the unity of the Holy Ghost, one God, world without end. Amen.

Communion. *Ps.* 44. Grace is poured abroad in thy lips: therefore hath God blessed thee forever and for ages of ages.

Postcommunion. Quickened by Thy heavenly Sacraments, we beseech Thee, O Lord our God, that through the intercession of blessed Anne, whom Thou didst choose to be the mother of her who brought forth Thy Son, we may become worthy to win eternal salvation. Through the same Lord Jesus Christ, Thy Son, who liveth and reigneth with Thee in the unity of the Holy Ghost, one God, world without end. Amen.

A PRAYER IN HONOR OF
THE BLESSED VIRGIN AND ST. ANNE

HAIL MARY, full of grace, the Lord is with thee, and may thy grace be with me! Blessed art thou among women, and blessed be St. Anne, thy mother who brought thee forth, O Virgin Mary, all immaculate, who didst give birth to Jesus Christ, the Son of the living God. Amen.

LITANY OF ST. ANNE
(For private use only.)

Lord, have mercy on us.
   Christ, have mercy on us.
Lord, have mercy on us. Christ, hear us.
   Christ, graciously hear us.
God the Father of Heaven,
   have mercy on us.
God the Son, Redeemer of the world,
   have mercy on us.
God the Holy Ghost,
   have mercy on us.
Holy Trinity, one God,
   have mercy on us.

Holy Mary, Queen of Angels and Saints,
   pray for us.
St. Anne, *pray for us.*
St. Anne, mother of Mary, the Queen of Heaven,
   pray for us.
St. Anne, instrument of the Holy Ghost,
   pray for us.
St. Anne, faithful spouse of St. Joachim,
   pray for us.
St. Anne, mirror of the married, *pray for us.*
St. Anne, example of widows, *pray for us.*
St. Anne, miracle of patience, *pray for us.*
St. Anne, mother of confidence, *pray for us.*
St. Anne, mother of constancy, *pray for us.*
St. Anne, mother of prayer, *pray for us.*
St. Anne, mother of blessing, *pray for us.*
St. Anne, vessel of sanctity, *pray for us.*
St. Anne, merciful mother, *pray for us.*
St. Anne, comfortress of the afflicted, *pray for us.*
St. Anne, help of the poor, *pray for us.*
St. Anne, protectress of virgins, *pray for us.*
St. Anne, support of the oppressed, *pray for us.*
St. Anne, refuge of thy clients, *pray for us.*

We sinners,
   We beseech thee, hear us.
Through thy love for Jesus and Mary,
   We beseech thee, hear us.

Through thy virtues and merits,
  We beseech thee, hear us.
Through thy goodness and mercy,
  We beseech thee, hear us.
Through thy compassion and charity,
  We beseech thee, hear us.
Through the graces bestowed on thee by God,
  We beseech thee, hear us.
Through the joys thou didst experience with Jesus and Mary,
  We beseech thee, hear us.
Through the happiness thou dost enjoy for all eternity,
  We beseech thee, hear us.
Through the honor given thee by the Saints in Heaven,
  We beseech thee, hear us.

Lamb of God, Who takest away the sins of the world, *Spare us, O Lord.*
Lamb of God, Who takest away the sins of the world, *Graciously hear us, O Lord.*
Lamb of God, Who takest away the sins of the world, *Have mercy on us.*

V. Pray for us, St. Anne,
R. That we may be made worthy of the promises of Christ.

Let Us Pray

O God, Who didst vouchsafe to endow blessed Anne with grace so that she might be worthy to become the mother of her who brought forth Thine only-begotten Son, mercifully grant that we who devoutly venerate her memory may also be helped by her powerful intercession. Through Christ our Lord. Amen.

NOVENA PRAYER TO ST. ANNE
To obtain some special favor

O GLORIOUS St. Anne, filled with compassion for those who invoke thee and with love for those who suffer, heavily laden with the weight of my troubles, I cast myself at thy feet and humbly beg of thee to take under thy special protection the present affair which I commend to thee. (*State your petition.*)

Be pleased to commend it to thy daughter, the Blessed Virgin Mary, and lay it before the throne of Jesus, so that He may bring it to a happy outcome. Cease not to intercede for me until my request is granted. Above all, obtain for me the grace of one day beholding my God face to face, and, with thee and Mary and all the Saints, of praising and blessing Him for all eternity. Amen.

Good St. Anne, mother of her who is our life, our sweetness and our hope, pray to her for us and obtain our request. (*three times*)

Good St. Anne, pray for us.

Jesus, Mary, Anne.

MEMORARE TO ST. ANNE
To obtain some special favor

REMEMBER, O holy mother St. Anne, that never was it known that anyone who fled to thy protection, implored thy help and sought thy intercession was left unaided, for thou art a most merciful mother and aid all who are in distress. Inspired with this confidence, I take refuge with thee and beseech thee, by thy great prerogative of being the mother of the Queen of Heaven and Grandmother of the Saviour of the world, come to my aid with thy powerful intercession, and obtain from thine Immaculate Daughter this favor (*mention it*). In honor of the nine months during which thou didst bear the ever-blessed Virgin in thy womb and brought her forth without stain of Original Sin, I now pray nine *Hail Marys*, which I offer thee through my Guardian Angel. Amen.

Hail Mary . . .(*nine times*)

PRAYER FOR GOD'S BLESSING ON THE MARRIED

I BLESS THEE, most gracious Lord Jesus Christ, for having ordained that Thy holy Mother, the Virgin Mary, of whom Thou, O Redeemer of all men, didst will to assume flesh, should proceed from the chaste union of Joachim and Anne. By Thy goodness I beseech Thee, through the merits of the holy parents Joachim and Anne, have mercy on (me and on) all who, in their memory, sanctify their life in the state of Matrimony. Give them rest and peace, health of body and soul; make them fruitful in good children, and after this exile, grant them eternal glory to Thy praise and honor, O sweetest and most gracious Saviour. Amen.

PRAYER FOR A WAYWARD CHILD

O HOLY MOTHER, St. Anne, so rich in graces! Thou wilt never leave unheard the pleadings and tears of a mother who invokes thee for a wayward child. Thou knowest my grief and the anguish of my heart. Look down with thy maternal eyes upon this poor erring child, and bring him (her) back upon the way of salvation, that he (she) may again serve God faithfully and thus obtain eternal happiness. Through Christ our Lord. Amen.

Hail Mary . . . (*three times*)

RECOMMENDATION TO ST. ANNE

HAIL, O illustrious St. Anne, blessed among women because thou hadst the happiness of bearing in thy womb the holy and immaculate Virgin Mary, Mother of God. I participate in the joy thou didst experience on giving birth to her and offering her in the Temple to the Eternal Father. I pray thee, good mother, to present me to thy well-beloved Daughter and to her Son, Jesus. Be my protectress and advocate with Jesus and Mary; be my intercessor, my refuge, my consolation. Amen.

DEVOTIONS IN HONOR OF
THE FIVE JOYS OF ST. ANNE

1. O most gracious St. Anne! I remind thee of the great dignity bestowed on thee by the Most High in choosing thee to be the mother of the Mother of God. By this grace, I beseech thee, obtain from God that I may be numbered among His elect. Amen. *Hail Mary . . .*

2. O most noble St. Anne! I remind thee of the great joy thou didst experience when the Angel appeared to thee and announced that thou wouldst conceive a daughter who would become the Mother of the Son of God. By this great joy, I beseech thee, obtain patience and spiritual joy for me in all my adversities. Amen. *Hail Mary . . .*

3. O most excellent St. Anne! I remind thee of the joy thou didst experience when thou didst bring forth the fruit of thy womb. By this great joy, I beseech thee, obtain God's grace and favor for me through thy daughter's Divine Son. Amen. *Hail Mary . . .*

4. O most happy St. Anne! I remind thee of the great joy thou didst experience when thou didst offer to God the Father thy daughter of three years in the Temple of Jerusalem. By this great joy, I beseech thee, obtain for me the grace to serve

God faithfully according to my state of life. Amen. *Hail Mary . . .*

5. O good St. Anne, worthy of all praise! I remind thee of the great joy which is thine in Heaven in beholding thy most loving daughter and all thy family. By this great joy, I beseech thee, assist me at the hour of my death, and aid me to attain life everlasting. Amen. *Hail Mary . . .*

DEVOTIONS IN HONOR OF THE FIVE SORROWS OF ST. ANNE

1. O blessed Anne, remember that grief which pierced thy heart when thou with thy God-fearing spouse, St. Joachim, wast innocently humiliated and despised on account of thy barrenness. By this bitter grief, I beseech thee, obtain for me patience and resignation in every adversity, and preserve me from the everlasting pains of Hell. Amen. *Hail Mary . . .*

2. O blessed Anne, remember that grief which pierced thy heart when thy holy spouse Joachim, impelled by the Holy Ghost, departed from thee and for a long time remained far away on a mountain. By this thy bitter grief, I beseech thee, obtain

for me patience and resignation in every adversity, and preserve me from the everlasting pains of Hell. Amen. *Hail Mary . . .*

3. O blessed Anne, remember that grief which pierced thy heart when thou didst hear that thy loving daughter Mary, her Divine Child and St. Joseph were obliged to flee into Egypt on account of Herod's cruelty. By this bitter grief, I beseech thee, obtain for me patience and resignation in every adversity, and preserve me from the everlasting pains of Hell. Amen. *Hail Mary . . .*

4. O blessed Anne, remember that grief which pierced thy heart when thou didst hear nothing of Jesus, Mary and Joseph for seven years and didst fear for their lives. By this thy bitter grief, I beseech thee, obtain for me patience and resignation in every adversity, and preserve me from the everlasting pains of Hell. Amen. *Hail Mary . . .*

5. O blessed Anne, remember the grief which pierced thy heart when thou wast informed by neighbors who returned home that Mary and Joseph had lost the Divine Child in Jerusalem and had returned thither to find Him. By this grief, I beseech thee, obtain for me patience and resignation in every adversity, and preserve me from the everlasting pains of Hell. Amen. *Hail Mary . . .*

If you have enjoyed this book, consider making your next selection from among the following . . .

Moments Divine—Before Bl. Sacrament *Reuter* 10.00
Raised from the Dead—400 Resurrection Miracles 18.50
Wonder of Guadalupe. *Johnston* 9.00
St. Gertrude the Great. 2.50
Mystical City of God. (abr.) *Agreda*. 21.00
Abortion: Yes or No? *Grady, M.D.* 3.00
Who Is Padre Pio? *Radio Replies Press* 3.00
What Will Hell Be Like? *St. Alphonsus* 1.50
Life and Glories of St. Joseph. *Thompson* 16.50
Autobiography of St. Margaret Mary 7.50
The Church Teaches. *Documents* 18.00
The Curé D'Ars. *Abbé Francis Trochu* 24.00
What Catholics Believe. *Lovasik* 6.00
Clean Love in Courtship. *Lovasik* 4.50
History of Antichrist. *Huchede*. 4.00
Self-Abandonment to Div. Prov. *de Caussade* 22.50
Canons & Decrees of the Council of Trent 16.50
Love, Peace and Joy. *St. Gertrude/Prévot* 8.00
St. Joseph Cafasso—Priest of Gallows. *St. J. Bosco* 6.00
Mother of God and Her Glorious Feasts. *O'Laverty*. . . . 15.00
Apologetics. *Glenn* 12.50
Isabella of Spain. *William Thomas Walsh* 24.00
Philip II. P.B. *William Thomas Walsh*. 37.50
Fundamentals of Catholic Dogma. *Ott*. 27.50
Creation Rediscovered. *Keane* 21.00
Hidden Treasure—Holy Mass. *St. Leonard* 7.50
St. Philomena. *Mohr* 12.00
St. Philip Neri. *Matthews*. 7.50
Martyrs of the Coliseum. *O'Reilly*. 21.00
Thirty Favorite Novenas 1.50
Devotion to Infant Jesus of Prague 1.50
On Freemasonry *(Humanum Genus)*. *Leo XIII* 2.50
Thoughts of the Curé D'Ars. *St. John Vianney* 3.00
Way of the Cross. *St. Alphonsus Liguori* 1.50
Way of the Cross. *Franciscan* 1.50
Magnificent Prayers. *St. Bridget of Sweden* 2.00
Conversation with Christ. *Rohrbach* 12.50
Douay-Rheims New Testament. 16.50
Life of Christ. 4 vols. P.B. *Emmerich*. 60.00
The Ways of Mental Prayer. *Lehodey*. 16.50

Prices subject to change.

Prices subject to change.